Dear Pa

Buckle up! You are about to join yc ... exciting journey. The destination? I...

Road to Reading will help you and your child get there. The program offers books at five levels, or Miles, that accompany children from their first attempts at reading to successfully reading on their own. Each Mile is paved with engaging stories and delightful artwork.

Getting Started
For children who know the alphabet and are eager to begin reading
• easy words   • fun rhythms   • big type   • picture clues

Reading With Help
For children who recognize some words and sound out others with help
• short sentences   • pattern stories   • simple plotlines

Reading On Your Own
For children who are ready to read easy stories by themselves
• longer sentences   • more complex plotlines   • easy dialogue

First Chapter Books
For children who want to take the plunge into chapter books
• bite-size chapters   • short paragraphs   • full-color art

Chapter Books
For children who are comfortable reading independently
• longer chapters   • occasional black-and-white illustrations

There's no need to hurry through the Miles. Road to Reading is designed without age or grade levels. Children can progress at their own speed, developing confidence and pride in their reading ability no matter what their age or grade.

So sit back and enjoy the ride—every Mile of the way!

Library of Congress Cataloging-in-Publication Data
Dino-roars / poems selected by Lee Bennett Hopkins ; illustrated by
Cynthia Fisher.
    p.   cm. — (Road to reading.   Mile 3)
Includes index.
Summary: A collection of twenty humorous poems about dinosaurs by such
writers as Jane Yolen, Madeleine Comora, and Philip Yates.
ISBN 0-307-26327-4
1. Dinosaurs—Juvenile poetry.   2. Extinct animals—Juvenile
poetry.   3. Children's poetry, American.   [1. Dinosaurs—Poetry.
2. Humorous poetry.   3. American poetry.]   I. Hopkins, Lee Bennett.
II. Fisher, Cynthia, ill.   III. Series.
PS595.E93D45   1999
811.008' 0362—dc21

                                                                98-41766
                                                                CIP
                                                                AC

A GOLDEN BOOK • New York
Golden Books Publishing Company, Inc. New York, New York 10106

ISBN: 0-307-26327-4   R MM

DINO-
ROARS

**poems selected by
Lee Bennett Hopkins**

**illustrations by
Cynthia Fisher**

Acknowledgments

Thanks are due to the following for works printed herein:

Curtis Brown, Ltd. for "Hide and Seek" "Once We Went A-Waltzing" "Welcome to Stego's Grill" by Rebecca Kai Dotlich. Copyright © 1999 by Rebecca Kai Dotlich; "A Dino-Welcome" "A Wish" by Lee Bennett Hopkins. Copyright © 1999 by Lee Bennett Hopkins; "Bones" by Jane Yolen. Copyright © 1999 by Jane Yolen; "The Dinosore" by Jane Yolen. Copyright © 1994 by Jane Yolen. Originally appeared in *How Beastly!* published by Boyds Mills Press. All reprinted by permission of Curtis Brown, Ltd.

Lee Bennett Hopkins for "The Way They Were" by Tom Robert Shields. Used by permission of Lee Bennett Hopkins for the author, who controls all rights.

Marian Reiner for "Questions For A Dinosaur" from *The Tigers Brought Pink Lemonade* by Patricia Hubbell. Copyright © 1988 by Patricia Hubbell; "Giant Supersaurus" by Sandra Liatsos. Copyright © 1999 by Sandra Liatsos. Both reprinted by permission of Marian Reiner for the authors.

Special thanks are also due to:

Sandra Gilbert Brüg for "Did Dinosaurs Talk?" and "Dinosaur Baseball"/ Madeleine Comora for "Manners"/ Constance Andrea Keremes for "Duckbill Ditty" "High Flier" and "Tidy Triceratops"/ Linda Kulp for "Saltopus"/ Lawrence Schimel for "Back-to-School Sale" and "Schoolhouse Rock"/ Philip Yates for "Mega-Ton Roommate." All used by permission of the individual authors, who control all rights.

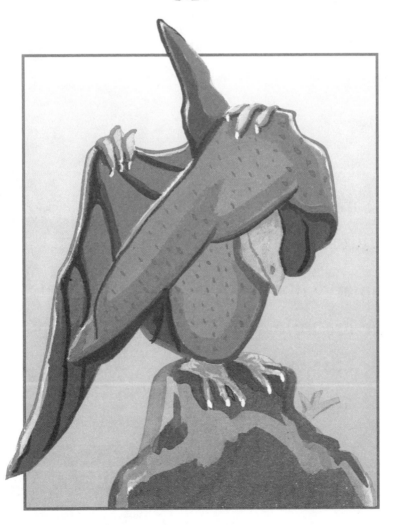

A DINO-WELCOME

by Lee Bennett Hopkins

Come—

read about

these mighty

creatures:

Some are silly,
Some are mild,
Some are gentle,
Some are wild.

Come—

read about
these
beasts of yore

in this
wondrous world
of
Dinosaur.

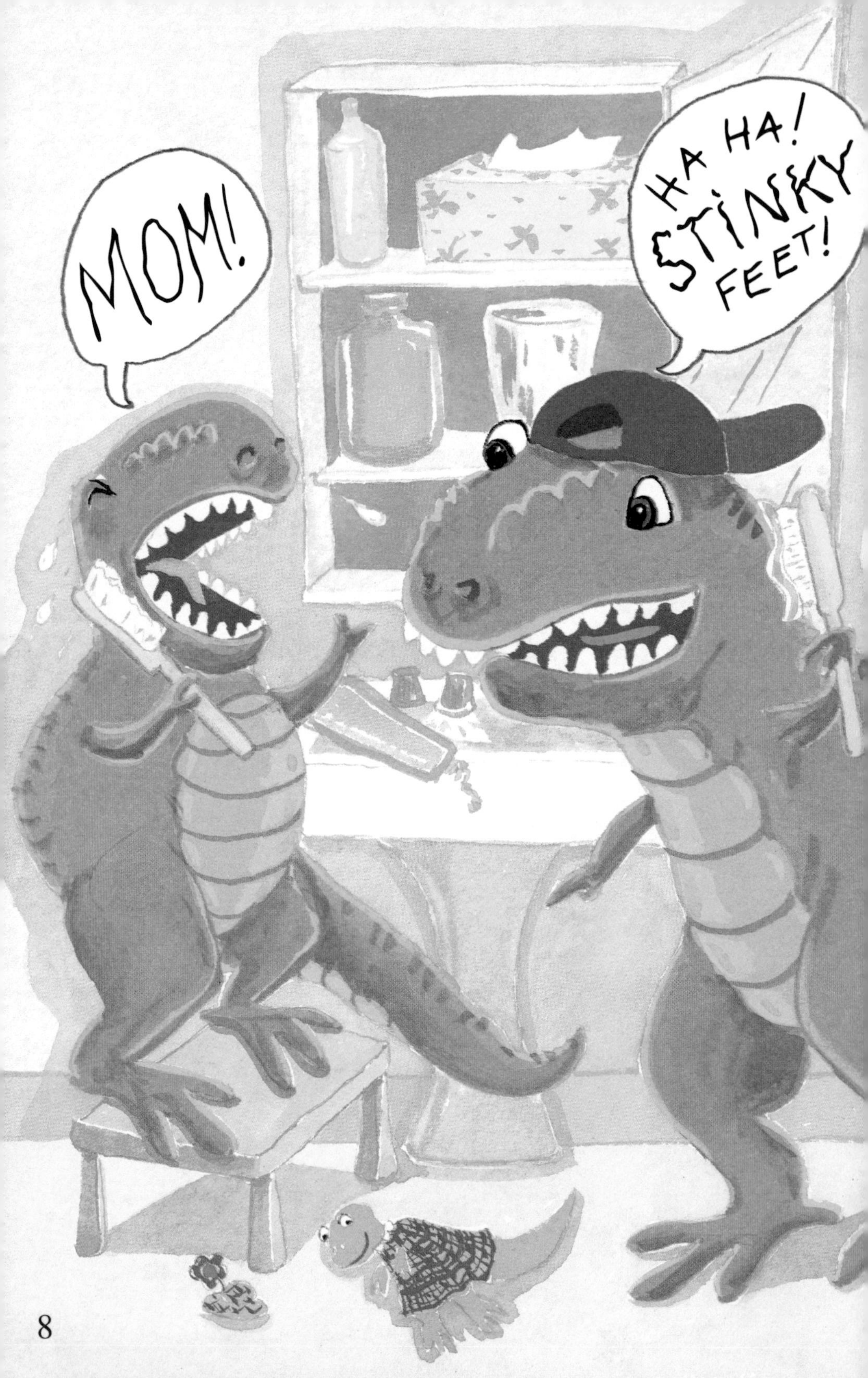
MOM!
HA HA! STINKY FEET!

DID DINOSAURS TALK?

by Sandra Gilbert Brüg

Did dinosaurs talk?

Did their scales fall off?

Did their big feet stink?

Were their tummies pink?

Did they ever blow their noses?

Was there dirt between their toeses?

Did dinosaurs play?

Do you think their mothers

Made them brush their teeth each day?

    NO WAY!

BACK-TO-SCHOOL SALE
by Lawrence Schimel

Clothes for every dinosaur,
No matter shape or size.
We have a wide selection.
You won't believe your eyes.

Shirts with room for spikes.
Pants with holes for tails.
Brontosaurus turtlenecks.
They're all on sale!

The hottest dino styles
For the hippest dinosaurs.
The latest fall fashions—
Now in DinoStores.

11

SCHOOLHOUSE ROCK

by Lawrence Schimel

I wonder if dinosaurs took P.E.

And went on field trip hikes.

And learned to add in algebra

By counting on their spikes.

Did they practice penmanship

And learn to write haiku?

Did dinos have to go to school

The way we humans do?

TIDY TRICERATOPS

by Constance Andrea Keremes

A horn's a handy thing to have,
    And three is even better.
I always have a place to hang
    My muffler and my sweater.

SALTOPUS

by Linda Kulp

I am Saltopus.

I am nasty and I'm mean.

My teeth are sharp as daggers.

My legs are strong and lean.

I dine on luscious lizards,

bugs are tasty snacks.

I am a mighty hunter—

and I'm ready to attack.

I am Saltopus.

My brain is rather small.

I could be a Dino King—

But I'm just one foot tall!

HIGH FLIER
by Constance Andrea Keremes

I'm a little Pterosaur,

Watch me spread my wings and soar.

Feather-light, I float and glide,

I'm better than an airplane ride.

DUCKBILL DITTY

by Constance Andrea Keremes

The Duckbill dino's pointy head
    Was like a built-in flute.

He did not talk.
He did not growl.

He just went:

    "TOOT!"

        "TOOT!"

            "TOOT!"

the Duckbill Doo-wops! ♪♪♪

A WISH
by Lee Bennett Hopkins

"HAPPY BIRTHDAY
   TO
   YOU!"

Sang a roaring
Dino-chorus.
"Now
   make
   a wish.

We've finished
our
song."

Micropachycephalosaurus
silently
thought:

Micro-
pachy-
cephal-
osaurus

"I wish
my name
wasn't
so
terribly
long!"

23

DINOSAUR BASEBALL

by Sandra Gilbert Brüg

A dino with a lumpy tail

Was good at hitting pitches.

The dino swung,

The bat went CRACK—

The baseball needed stitches.

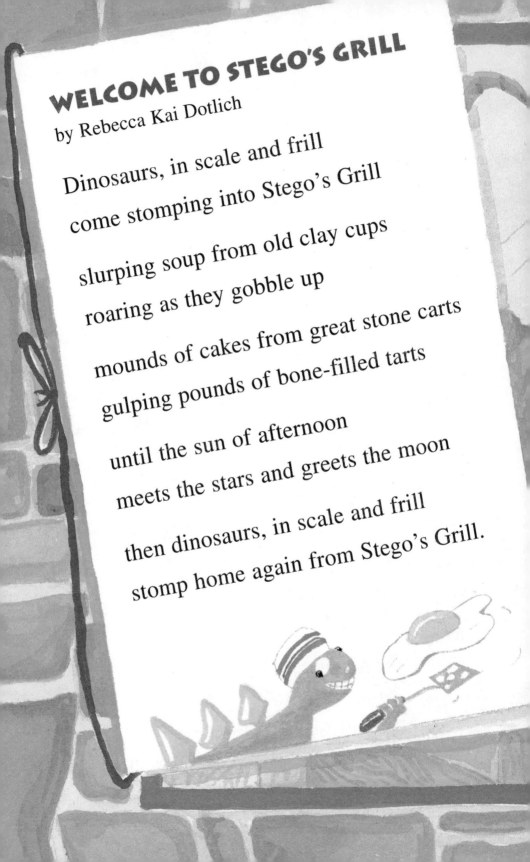

WELCOME TO STEGO'S GRILL

by Rebecca Kai Dotlich

Dinosaurs, in scale and frill
come stomping into Stego's Grill

slurping soup from old clay cups
roaring as they gobble up

mounds of cakes from great stone carts
gulping pounds of bone-filled tarts

until the sun of afternoon
meets the stars and greets the moon

then dinosaurs, in scale and frill
stomp home again from Stego's Grill.

THE DINOSORE

by Jane Yolen

Poor Dinosore, his body's big,

His tail it weighs a ton,

His head is full of bones and stones,

And when he tries to run

The pounding poundage gets him down.

He gasps and gasps some more.

His aching feet, they have him beat,

That's why he's Dinosore.

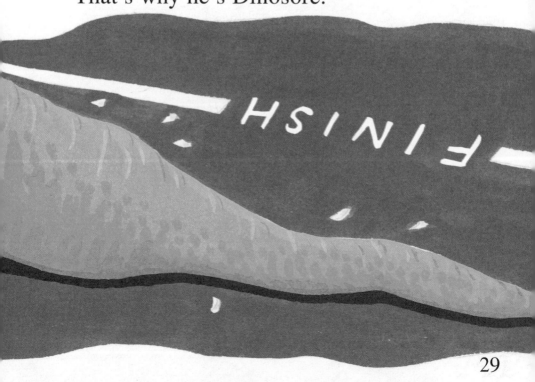

GIANT SUPERSAURUS

by Sandra Liatsos

Giant Supersaurus
never thought the storms
were frightening.

He opened up his mouth
and used his teeth
to catch the lightning.

32

MANNERS

by Madeleine Comora

When T-Rex asks his friends to dine,

They try to be polite,

But when they see the way he eats

They lose their appetite.

HIDE AND SEEK

by Rebecca Kai Dotlich

The air is still,

the stars are bright,

as dinos hide

and seek tonight.

Scaled feet

and lizard knees

go pounding through

the shrubs and trees;

holding breath

and squeezing eyes—

it's hard to hide because of size!

MEGA-TON ROOMMATE

by Philip Yates

If I shared my room with a Brachiosaur,

And we had a bunk bed for two,

The creature would sleep

on the bottom for sure,

And I'd sleep on top...wouldn't you?

ONCE WE WENT A-WALTZING

by Rebecca Kai Dotlich

Once we went a-waltzing,

our steps were steep and grand,

we kicked our knees

by ancient seas—

we stomped our prints in sand.

Once we went a-waltzing,

for years we swayed and swirled,

we dipped our scales

and twirled our tails—

when once we owned the world.

QUESTIONS FOR A DINOSAUR

by Patricia Hubbell

O Stegosaurus,
  if you saw us,
  would you be
  against or for us?

Would you shout,
  "Hooray, we're linked!"
  Or would you wish
  we were extinct?

THE WAY THEY WERE

Tom Robert Shields

We'll never know
Dinosaurs
The way they were
Back when.

Did they say:

    Aloha-saurus!

    Adios-saurus!

    Arriverderci-saurus!

Or

    Farewell?
Before
we
knew,
we
    lost-o-saurus
    them.

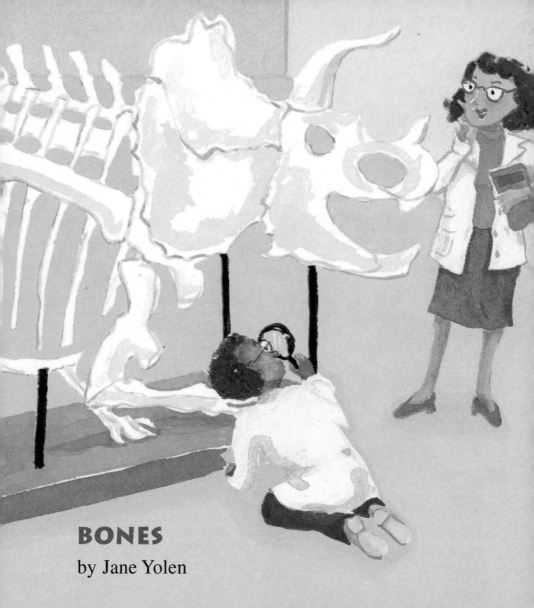

BONES
by Jane Yolen

Bones, bones, dinosaur bones,
Not for the soup pot
    because they are stones.
Not for the dog to chew, not for the cat,
Only for scientists to wonder at.

HOW TO SAY

BRACHIOSAUR
(BRAK-ee-o-sawr)

BRONTOSAURUS
(bron-to-SAWR-us)

MICROPACHYCEPHALOSAURUS
(my-kro-pak-ee-sef-ah-lo-sawr-us)

PTEROSAUR
(TAYR-o-sawr)

THEIR NAMES

SALTOPUS
(SAHLT-o-pus)

STEGOSAURUS
(steg-o-SAWR-us)

SUPERSAURUS
(su-per-SAWR-us)

TRICERATOPS
(try-SAHR-ah-tops)

T-REX OR TYRANNOSAURUS
(ty-ran-o-SAWR-us)

INDEX OF AUTHORS AND TITLES